Seasons and You

SUMMER

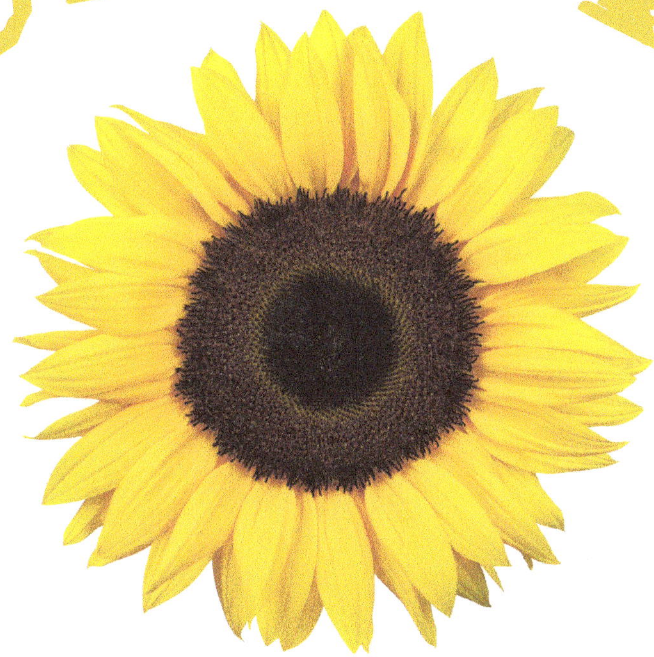

By Shalini Vallepur

Published in 2023 by **KidHaven Publishing, an Imprint of Greenhaven Publishing, LLC**
29 East 21st Street
New York, NY 10010

Edited by: John Wood

Designed by: Danielle Webster-Jones

Cataloging-in-Publication Data

Names: Vallepur, Shalini.
Title: Summer / Shalini Vallepur.
Description: New York : KidHaven Publishing, 2023. | Series: Seasons and you | Includes glossary and index.
Identifiers: ISBN 9781534541375 (pbk.) | ISBN 9781534541399 (library bound) | ISBN 9781534541382 (6 pack) | ISBN 9781534541405 (ebook)
Subjects: LCSH: Summer--Juvenile literature.
Classification: LCC QB637.6 V35 2023 | DDC 508.2--dc23

Manufactured in the United States of America

CPSIA compliance information: Batch #CSKH23: For further information contact Greenhaven Publishing LLC, New York, New York at 1-844-317-7404.

Please visit our website, www.greenhavenpublishing.com. For a free color catalog of all our high-quality books, call toll free 1-844-317-7404 or fax 1-844-317-7405.

Find us on

IMAGE CREDITS

All images are courtesy of Shutterstock.com, unless otherwise specified. With thanks to Getty Images, Thinkstock Photo and iStockphoto. Cover & throughout – Ami Parikh, Jomic, Hayati Kayhan, gilotyna4, Shebeko, Nadia Cruzova, FeelIFree, Mr. SUTTIPON YAKHAM, Kleber Cordeiro, Markus Mainka, Africa Studio, irin-k, Africa Studio, Carolyn Franks, NYS, thananya, TinasDreamworld, Yellow Cat, GalapagosPhoto, schankz, guaho. 4 – GOLFX. 5 – herle_catharina. 6 – AnnGaysorn. 7 – rattiya lamrod, G.roman. 8 – Deborah Kolb. 9 – Bell nipon, Daleen Loest, Kidsada Manchinda, Anton Starikov. 10 – Shairaa. 11 – Giftography. 12 – FamVeld. 13 – BonD80. 14 – Kirsanov Valeriy Vladimirovich. 15 – MRS. NUCH SRIBUANOY. 16 – Julia Zavalishina. 17 – cynoclub. 18 – Nataliia Sokolovskaia. 19 – Guiderom. 20 – Zhangmoon618, CC BY-SA 3.0 <https://creativecommons.org/licenses/by-sa/3.0>, via Wikimedia Commons. 21 – stockyimages. 22-23 – Honza Krej.

CONTENTS

Words that look like this can be found in the glossary on page 24.

SUMMER!

Summer is here! Summer is a season. Most places in the world have four seasons. Each one has different weather.

Spring, summer, autumn, and winter are the four seasons.

Summer comes after spring.

Some places around the world do not have these seasons. Some places only have two seasons: rainy and dry.

SUMMER WEATHER

It is usually warm in summer. The days can be very long. In some places, the sun stays out at night!

In summer there can be thunderstorms with thunder, lightning, and rain. Hurricanes with lots of strong winds can happen in some places.

FUN IN THE SUN!

It can be very sunny in summer! We must protect our bodies from the sun. We can do this by wearing the right things and not staying in the sun for too long.

On hot summer days, make sure you drink a lot of water. You should drink six to eight glasses of water a day.

PLANTS IN SUMMER

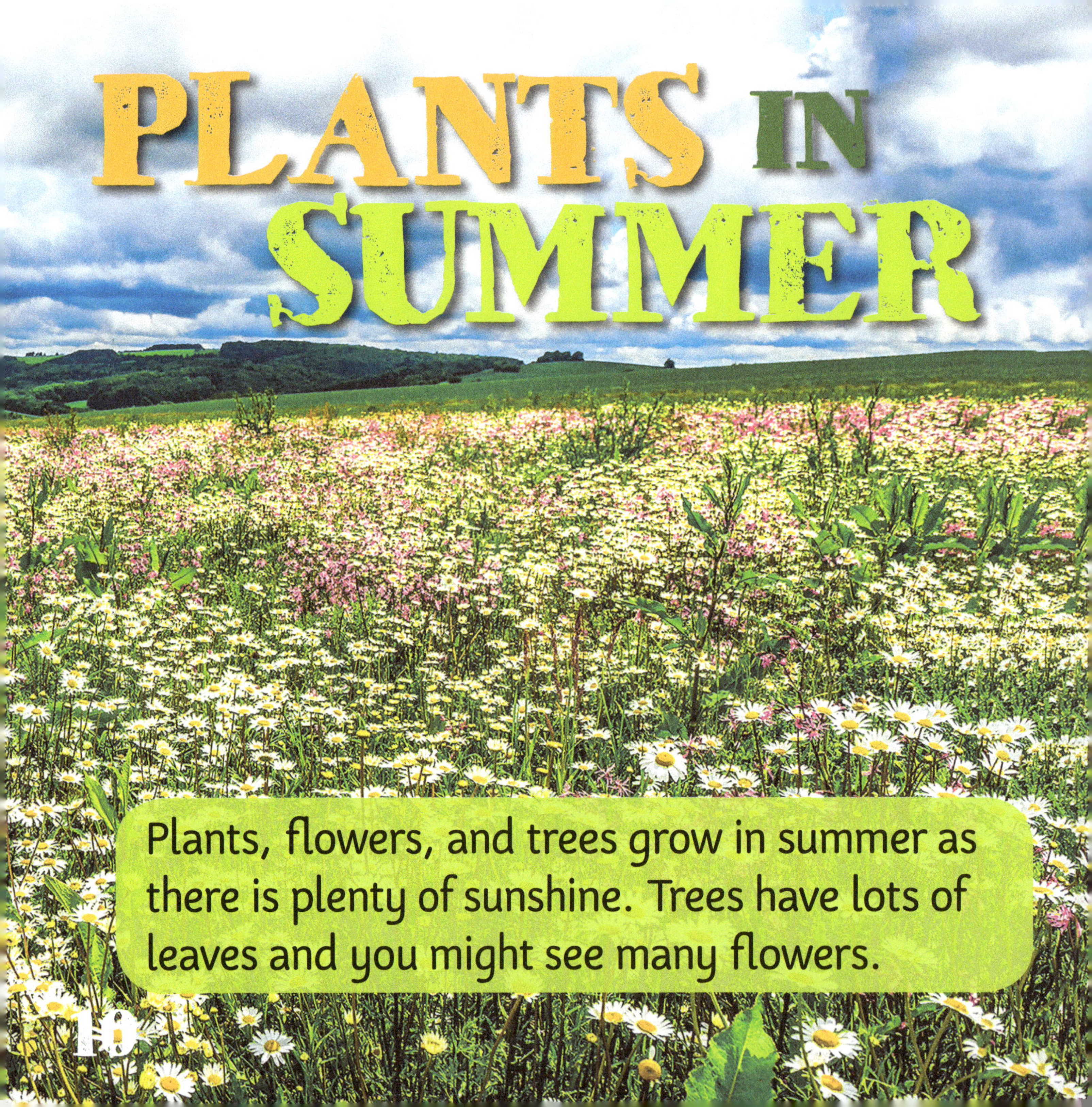

Plants, flowers, and trees grow in summer as there is plenty of sunshine. Trees have lots of leaves and you might see many flowers.

In some parts of the world, summer can be very hot with little rain. Plants in the desert, such as cacti, keep water inside them for when there is little rain.

Summer in the desert is very hot!

Many fruits and vegetables become ripe in summer, which means they are ready to eat. They are then harvested. Strawberries are a fruit that is in season during summer.

Many people enjoy strawberry picking during summer.

Melons are also in season in summer. They grow best in warmer countries. There are lots of different types of melons.

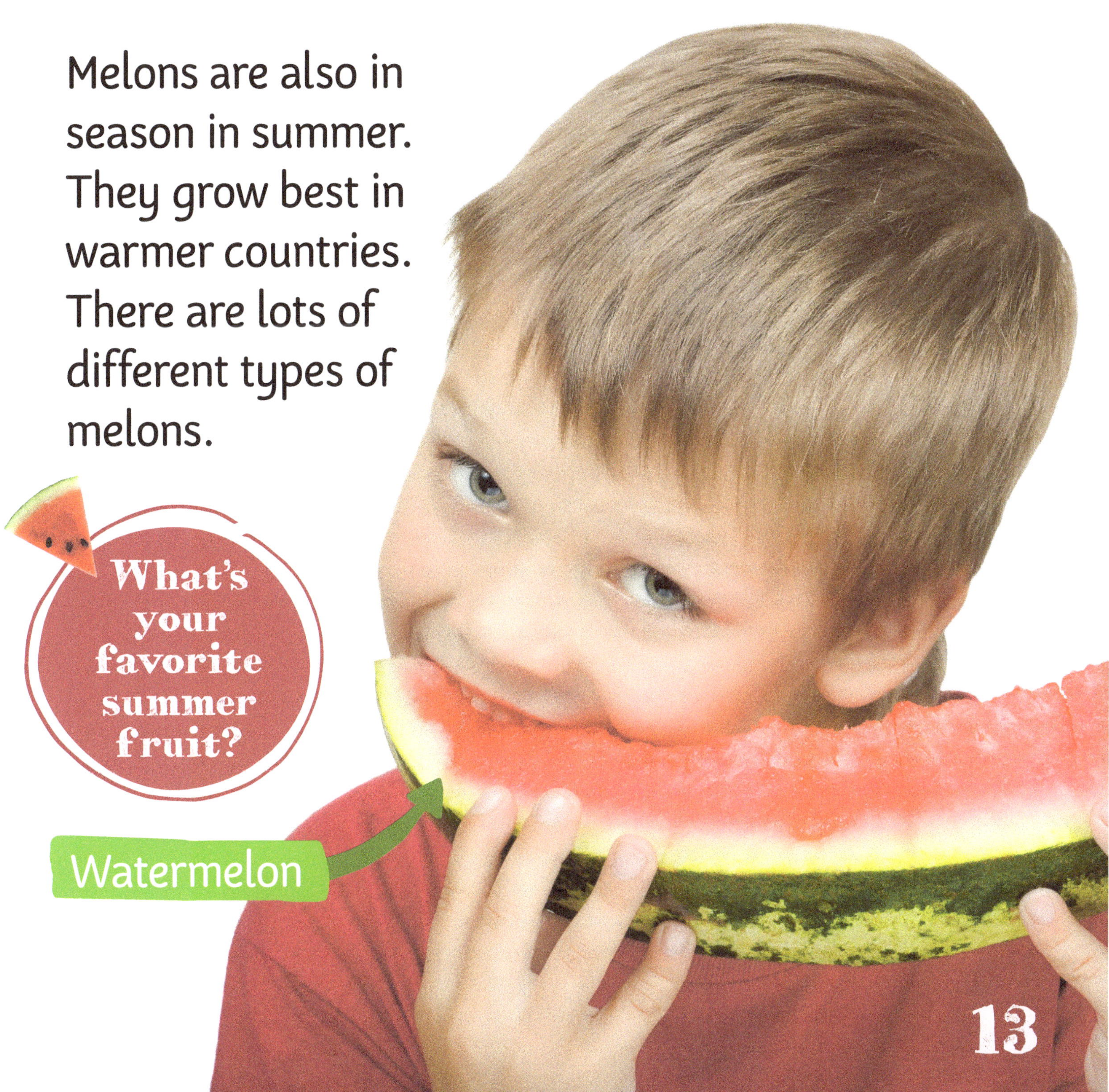

ANIMALS IN SUMMER

Lots of different bugs and insects can be seen in summer. They feed on the many plants and flowers. Snails love eating cabbages in the summer, especially if it rains.

Grasshoppers often eat leaves.

Bees and butterflies get food from flowers. They drink the nectar from flowers. Summer is a very busy time for them!

Have you ever seen a butterfly drinking from a flower?

Some animals, such as dogs and cats, molt during summer. This means that they lose some of their fur to keep cool.

This sheep has been shorn. This means it will be nice and cool during summer. The farmer sells the wool.

Why do you think animals need to molt or be shorn?

TIME TO CELEBRATE!

There are lots of festivals in summer around the world. The summer solstice happens during summer on the longest day of the year.

In the UK, people gather at Stonehenge for the summer solstice. This is usually around June 21. They watch the sunset and the sunrise.

In some countries, people celebrate the summer solstice with bonfires.

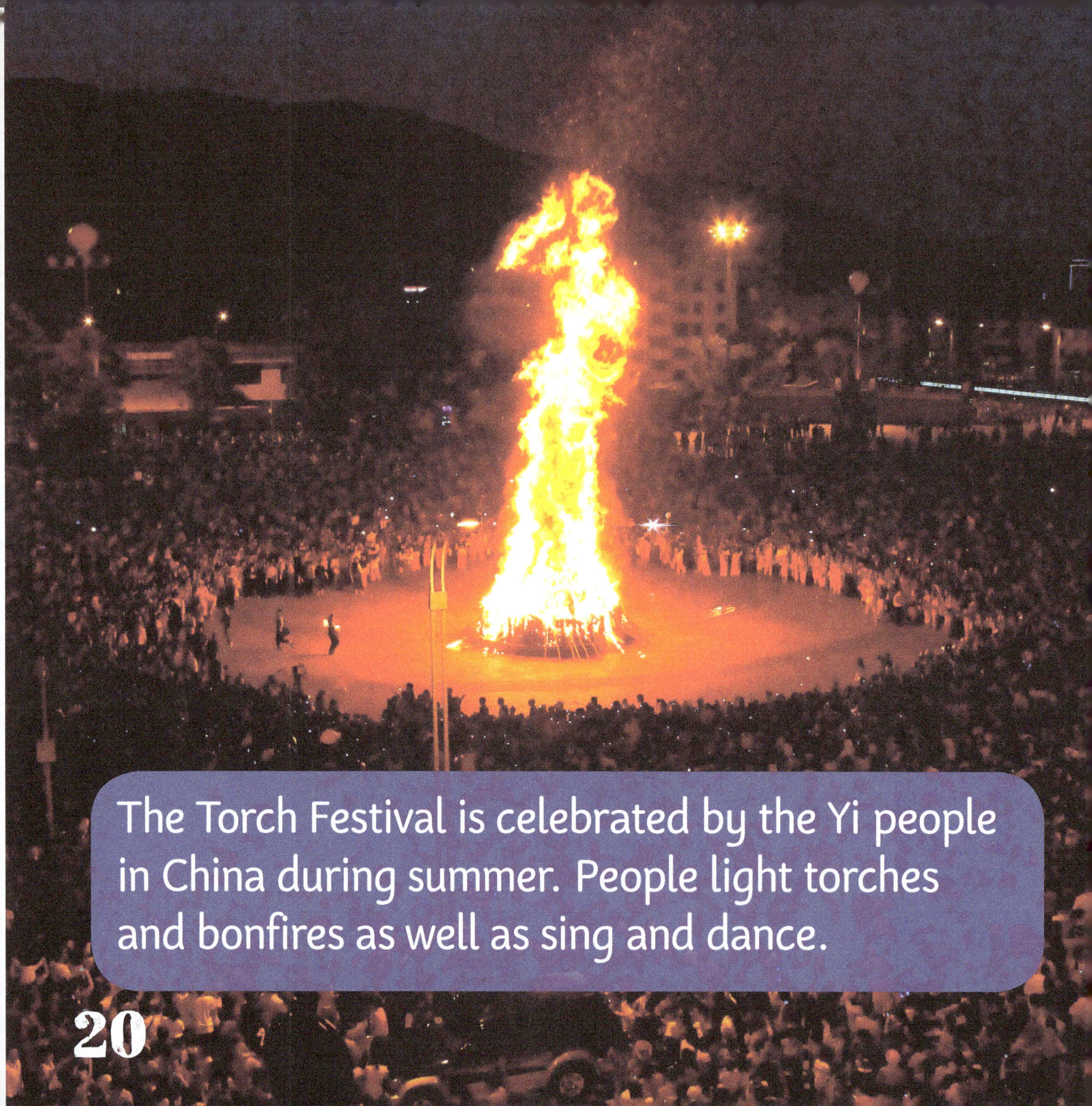

The Torch Festival is celebrated by the Yi people in China during summer. People light torches and bonfires as well as sing and dance.

The Wianki Festival is celebrated in Poland. People make garlands to wear on their heads and light fireworks at night.

You might celebrate the Fourth of July in summer!

THE END OF SUMMER

Summer happens at different times of the year around the world, but it is usually a season with sunshine and warmth.

What's your favorite thing about summer?

Towards the end of summer, the days start to get shorter and a little colder. It isn't long before autumn arrives!

GLOSSARY

bonfires	large fires that are built to celebrate something
celebrate	to do something special for an important event
festivals	special times of the year when people come together to remember or do something
garlands	large loops made of flowers or leaves that can be worn or hung up
harvested	when fully grown crops have been picked
hurricanes	strong storms with winds that move in a circle
in season	when a plant grows best
nectar	a sweet liquid made by plants
protect	to look after something
shorn	when fur or hair has been cut off

INDEX